G000049602

A

WITH JESUS

Compiled by

Patrick O'Mara, S.J.

Messenger Publications

Published by
Messenger Publications,
37, Lower Leeson Street,
Dublin 2.

Cover phototograph ©: *Dia Dienst.*

Nihil Obstat: Joannes J. Coyne, S.J.
                     Cens. Theol. Dep.
Imprimi Potest: + Eduardus,
                     Archiep. Dublinen.
                     Hib. Primas.
Dublini: die 30 Octobris, 1929.

                10-6-90
                3-12-92
                5-1-94
                6-6-97
                1-5-00

        ISBN 1 872245 30 7

FOREWORD

In the year 1675, our divine Lord said to Saint Margaret Mary: 'Behold the heart which has loved so much. It has spared nothing... while in acknowledgement I get back nothing for the most part but ingratitude, contempt, irreverence, sacrileges and coldness'.

What was true in 1675, is also true today.

The hearts of many are turned from God. They have no time for him. They forget his love. They forget that they depend on him for all.

Even when the churches fill and Christ offers himself to God in the sacrifice of the Mass for the sins and needs of us all, our hearts are cold and unresponsive.

Perhaps this little book, with its simple prayers, may help someone to thank Jesus for his wonderful love, to linger with him longer in reparation and to offer him a heart's devoted love.

1st QUARTER

ADORATION, TRUST, THANKSGIVING
OFFERING OF THE HOLY HOUR

My most sweet Jesus, I wish during this hour to
watch with you, and with the love of my heart to
console you for the bitter sorrow which over-
whelmed you in the Garden of Gethsemani. I want
to forget myself and all that concerns me, except
my sins. I was a cause of sorrow to you then, now
I want to comfort you. I offer you this hour of
prayer and reparation, for the conversion of people
and of nations and for every other intention for
which you suffered and died. Help me to pass this
Holy Hour that I may promote your interest
throughout the world.

ASPIRATION OF SAINT MARGARET MARY

O Heart of love, I place my trust in you for though
I fear all things from my weakness, I hope all things
from your mercy.

'No one ever hoped in the Lord and was reject-
ed.' God's promise! *(Ecclus 2:11).*

O Jesus Christ, my Lord and my Redeemer, I
will trust in your Sacred Heart for ever and ever.

My God, I believe in you because you are Trust
itself; I hope in you because you are infinitely good;
I love you because your are infinitely loveable, and
I love my neighbour as myself for love of you.

Sacred Heart of Jesus, I place my trust in you.

GOD ALONE

No one worth serving, but God;
No one so tender, so grateful.
No one worth trusting, but God:
No friend so unchanging, so faithful.
No one worth loving, but God;
No heart holds his wealth of affection,
No one worth seeking, but God -
In his exquisite, endless perfection.

Kathleen Donegan

ACT OF CONFIDENCE IN GOD
By Saint Claude la Colombiére, S.J.

My God! I firmly believe that you watch over all your creatures and that we can want for nothing while we trust in you. I have decided from now on to cast away all my worries and to place my confidence in you.

'In peace I lie down and at once fall asleep, for it is you and none other, Lord, who makes me rest secure' (*Ps 4:8*).

I may be deprived of health and honour; sickness may take from me the best means of serving you; I may even lose your grace by sin; but through your help I will never lose my hope in you. I will preserve it in spite of evil to the end of my life.

Others may look for happiness from their riches or their talents; they may trust to the innocence of their lives, or to the rigour of their penance, to the number of their good works, or to the fervour of their prayers; but all my confidence shall be placed in you.

I know well that I am weak and changeable; I know the power of temptation over the most perfect. As long as I hope in you I have nothing to fear from my enemies, and as my confidence is placed in you, I shall never cease to hope. I know that I cannot hope too much in you and that I cannot obtain less than I hope for from you.

I hope that you will protect me against all future dangers. I hope that you will always love me and that I shall love you daily more and more.

THE IRISH 'TE DEUM'

Thanks be to God for the light and the darkness;
Thanks be to God for the hail and the snow;
Thanks be to God for shower and sunshine;
Thanks be to God for all things that grow;
Thanks be to God for lightning and tempest;
Thanks be to God for fortune and woe;
Thanks be to God for his own great goodness;
Thanks be to God for what is, is so;
Thanks be to God when the harvest is plenty;
Thanks be to God when the barn is low;
Thanks be to God when our pockets are empty;
Thanks be to God when again they o'erflow;
Thanks be to God when the Mass bell and steeple
Are heard and are seen throughout Erin's green isle;

Thanks be to God that the priest and the people
Are ever united in danger and trial;
Thanks be to God that the brave sons of Erin
Have the faith of their fathers as lively as aye;
Thanks be to God that Erin's fair daughters
Press close after Mary on heaven's highway.

THANKSGIVING

O my God, I thank you for all the favours you have
bestowed on me. I give you thanks from the bottom
of my heart for having created me... for all the joys
of life and for all the sorrows... for the home you
gave me and for all the love that surrounded me in
my home... for the friends I have made through life.

My Lord God, I thank you for guarding me
always and keeping me safe. I thank you for for-
giving me so often and so easily in the Sacrament
of Reconciliation, for offering yourself in the Holy
Mass, for coming from heaven to me in Holy
Communion, in spite of the coldness of my wel-
come, for your patient waiting in the Sacrament of
the Altar.

My Jesus, I thank you for having lived and
worked and died for me. I thank you for your love.
I thank you, Lord, for preparing a place in heaven
for me, where I hope to be happy with you and to
thank you.

You have dealt very generously and very ten-
derly with me; I cannot hope to thank you as I

should; but, with your help, my future life will be one long thanksgiving. I beg your sweet Mother Mary to thank you for me out of her heart of hearts for your gift of love to me.

PRAYER

If you want for me to be in darkness, I thank you; if you want me to be in light, I thank you again. If you promise to comfort me, I thank you; and if it is your will that I be afflicted, I thank you again.

ADORATION

Jesus, my Lord and my God, Son of God and Son of the Virgin Mary, I believe that you are here and I adore you... Behind the whiteness of the Sacred Host, I believe that you are present, in perfect, glorious manhood, and I adore you... With the angels of your court, I kneel in humble adoration... With all your saints, your poor servant adores you... With your holy Mother Mary, I kneel here in humble adoration.

TRUST

My Lord and my God, I believe all that you have ever taught us. It is hard for me to believe that you can love someone as sinful as I am; but I do.

I believe that your love for me is not a passing one; 'You have loved me with an everlasting love',

9

and, therefore, O Sacred Heart of Jesus, I place all my trust in you.

I believe your love for me is as tender as a mother's love, and, therefore, O Sacred Heart of Jesus, I place all my trust in you.

I believe you have planned everything that shall ever happen to me, lovingly and wisely, and, therefore, O Sacred Heart of Jesus, I place all my trust in you.

I will never seek things forbidden by you because you know what is best for me.

I will always pray, 'May your holy will be done in all things', because I trust in you, O Sacred Heart of Jesus.

I will accept the crosses of life, as I accept the joys, with a grateful heart, because I trust in you, O Sacred Heart of Jesus.

I will not be worried or anxious about anything, because I trust in you, O Sacred Heart of Jesus.

I will never lose heart in my efforts to be good, because I trust in you, O Sacred Heart of Jesus.

However weak or sinful I may be, I will never doubt your mercy, because I trust in you, O Sacred Heart of Jesus.

O Sacrament most holy,
O Sacrament divine,
All praise and all thanksgiving
Be every moment thine.

2nd QUARTER

PETITION

There's a wideness in God's mercy
  Like the wideness of the sea;
There's a kindness in his justice
  Which is more than clemency.
There is no place where earth's sorrows
  Are more felt, than up in heaven;
There's no place where earth's failings
  Have such kind judgement given.
For the love of God is broader
  Than the measures of our mind.
And the heart of the Eternal
  Is most wonderfully kind.
But we make his love too narrow
  By false limits of our own,
And we magnify his strictness
  With a zeal he will not own.
If our love were but more simple.
  We should take him at his word;
And our lives would be all sunshine
  In the sweetness of our Lord.

Fr Faber

PRAYER

My loving Lord! A thousand welcomes! O Son of Mary, I love you; indeed I do. Who am I at all, that you should come next or near me? O God of heaven, make a little corner for me in your heart, and never while there is life in me let me lose my place there and after death may I still hide there. Amen.

11

PRAYER

My Lord and my God, you have said that anything we ask the Father in your name he will give. Relying on this promise - the promise of the God of truth - we ask our heavenly Father now for what we want. We ask it in the name of his only begotten Son, Jesus Christ, provided it is for our good, and his greater glory. Amen.

(Here recall what it is you most desire from God. Pray also for the gift of dying in the state of grace.)

THE ANSWER IS SURE

The time may be delayed, the manner may be unexpected, but the answer is sure to come. Not a tear of sacred sorrow, not a breath of holy desire, poured out in prayer to God, will ever be lost.

PRAYERS

O Lord Almighty, you allow evil only because you can turn it into good for us. Hear our humble prayers and grant that we may remain faithful to you until death. Grant us, also, the strength to do your most holy will.

May the most just, most high and most adorable will of God be in all things done, praised and magnified for ever.

O Lord Jesus, be not my Judge but my Saviour. Jesus in the Blessed Sacrament, have mercy on us.

Divine Heart of Jesus, convert sinners, save the dying, set free the holy souls in purgatory.

Lord, reward with eternal life all those who do us good, for your name's sake. Amen.

My Jesus, mercy!

O Heart of Jesus, burning with love for us, inflame our hearts with love of you.

ASPIRATIONS TO THE HEART OF JESUS

Heart of Jesus, who has borne all our griefs, strengthen me.

Heart of Jesus, who has weighed this sorrow before sending it to us, help me.

Heart of Jesus, ever touched by the sight of sorrow, pity me.

Heart of Jesus, beautiful in your sorrows, teach me to become holy by means of this affliction.

Heart of Jesus, spending yourself for souls in the midst of your sorrows, make me unselfish in bearing mine.

Heart of Jesus, troubled at the grave of Lazarus, comfort those who mourn.

Heart of Jesus, touched with compassion at the widow's tears, have pity on those who mourn.

Heart of Jesus, softened by the tears of Magdalene, pity the sorrowful.

Heart of Jesus, whose sorrow was ever before you, teach us to unite our griefs to yours.

Heart of Jesus, who suffered the agony of Gethsemani, strengthen us in all the sorrows of life.

Heart of Jesus, whose unknown agonies we shall know and love in heaven, teach us to suffer alone with God for his glory.

Heart of Jesus, broken with love and sorrow on the cross, draw us to yourself in our sorrows, and make us faithful to the end. Amen.

A UNIVERSAL PRAYER

O my God, I believe in you: strengthen my faith. All my hopes are in you; you enable me to realise them. I love you with my whole heart; teach me to love you daily more and more. I am sorry that I have offended you; please forgive me. I adore you as my first beginning. I aspire after you as my constant benefactor. I call upon you as my sovereign protector.

O God, guide me by your wisdom, restrain me by the thought of your justice, comfort me by your mercy, defend me by your power.

To you I desire to consecrate all my thoughts, words, actions and sufferings, that from now on I may think of you, speak of you, willingly refer all my actions to your greater glory, and carry willingly whatever cross you ask me to bear.

Lord, I desire that in all things your will may be done, because it is your will, and may it be done in the manner you wish.

Fill my heart with tender affection for your goodness, hatred for my faults and love for my neighbour.

Let me always remember to be submissive to your will, kind to my neighbours, faithful to my friends and charitable to my enemies.

Teach me, God, about the greatness of heaven, the shortness of time and the length of eternity.

Grant that I may prepare for death, that I may fear your judgements, that I may escape hell and in the end obtain heaven, through the merits of our Lord Jesus Christ. Amen.

ANIMA CHRISTI

Soul of Christ, sanctify me,
Body of Christ, save me,
Blood of Christ, enliven me,
Water flowing from the side of Christ,
Wash me.
Passion of Christ, strengthen me,
O good Jesus, hear me,
Within your wounds, hide me,
Never let me be separated from you.
From every evil, defend me.
At the hour of death, call me,
And bid me come to you,
That with your saints I may praise you,
For all eternity. Amen.

PRAYER TO THE SACRED HEART
By Saint Claude la Colombiére, S.J.

O Sacred Heart of Jesus, teach me to be less concerned with myself since there is no other way of knowing you. Grant that I may do nothing that is not worthy of you. Teach me what I ought to do to attain to your love.

I feel in myself a great wish to please you and a great inability to do so, without a special light and assistance which I can look for only from you. Accomplish your will, O Lord, in me. I oppose it, I know; but I would prefer not to do so. It is for you, O divine heart of Jesus, to do all. You alone shall have the glory if I become a saint and it is for this alone that I desire to be perfect. Amen.

PRAYER FOR A FRIEND

May the grace and blessing of the Sacred Heart be
with you;
The peace of the Sacred Heart encompass you;
The merits of the Sacred Heart plead for you;
The love of the Sacred Heart inflame you;
The sorrows of the Sacred Heart console you;
The virtues of the Sacred Heart shine forth in every
word and work;
May almighty God shelter you under the shadow of
his wings;
And may the joys of heaven be your eternal
reward. Amen

ST. PATRICK'S PRAYER

May the strength of God guide me this day, and
may his power preserve me.
May the wisdom of God instruct me; the eye of
God watch over me; the ear of God hear me; the
word of God give sweetness to my speech; the
hand of God defend me; and may I follow in the
way of God.

    Christ be with me, Christ before me,
    Christ be after me, Christ within me,
    Christ beneath me, Christ above me,
    Christ at my right hand, Christ at my left,
    Christ in the fort, Christ in the chariot,
    Christ in the ship;
    Christ in the heart of every one who thinks of me,
    Christ in the mouth of every one who speaks of me,
    Christ in every eye that sees me,
    Christ in every ear that hears me.

REPARATION
Translation of Ancient Irish Verses

    I offer you
Every flower that ever grew,
Every bird that ever flew,
Every wind that ever blew,
   Good God!
Every thunder rolling,
Every church bell tolling,
Every leaf and sod.
   Laudamus Te!

    I offer you
Every wave that ever moved,
Every heart that ever loved,
God, your Father's well-beloved,
   Dear Lord!
Every river dashing,
Every lightning flashing,
Like and angel's sword.
   Benedicimus Te!

    I offer you
Every cloud that ever swept
O'er the skies, and broke and wept
In rain, and with flow'rets slept,
   My king!
Each communicant praying,
Every angel staying
Before your throne to sing.
   Adoramus Te!

I offer you
Every flake of virgin snow,
Every spring the earth below,
Every human joy and woe,
   My love!
O Lord! And all your glorious
Self, o'er death victorious,
Throned in heaven above.
   Glorificamus Te!

Take all of them, O darling Lord,
In your blessed Sacrament loved, adored,
Multiply each and every one,
Make each of them into millions -
   Into glorious millions,
   Into gorgeous millions,
Of Glorias, glorious Son!.
And then, O dear Lord, listen,
Where the tabernacles glisten,
To those praises, holiest One!

RESOLUTIONS

Pause for a moment... listen: He, our friend, with whom we have been pleading, is asking for something. Do not refuse him, give him generously what he wants. Is it to give up a sinful habit? Is it to relinquish some pleasure? To be more kind in speech, more patient, more humble?.... Promise him now, and let your resolutions be the proof of your desire to love him more and more, to respond to his divine inspirations, and to atone for your past coldness and neglect.

Dearest Jesus, teach us to be generous.
Teach us to love and serve you as you deserve.
To give and not to count the cost;
To fight and not to heed the wounds;
To toil and not to seek for rest;
To labour and to look for no reward,
Save that of knowing that we do
Your holy will. Amen.

(Now, go over in your mind the resolutions you intend, with God's help, to keep, concerning your prayers, the reception of the sacraments, the avoidance of sin, the occasions of sin, your daily duties, etc. There is no better way of consoling the Sacred Heart for the coldness of the sins of other years.)

PRAYER

O Jesus, divine friend and lover, we promise to serve you in the future in active love. Mere words are worth little if our lives displease you. We promise to be more attentive to our prayers, to be more regular and fervent in our reception of you in Holy Communion and to avoid giving you deliberate offence again. We are weak and unstable but help us, O Lord Jesus, to make you reparation for the past, and to console you during our future lives for all your Sacred Heart has suffered.

ACTS OF REPARATION OF ST GERTRUDE

Most sweet Jesus, I give thanks to you and bless you, by the heart of all rational beings, in reparation for all the blasphemies, for all the outrages, heaped upon you here on earth.

I bless you for every sigh, for every tear, for every sorrow you endured.

I bless you for every drop of blood you shed in your passion, for every blow you got, for every grief you felt.

I bless you for every step you took along that road of suffering, for every time your strength gave out.

I bless you for every wound inflicted on you by the cruel scourges, for every thorn that pierced your brow, for every time your sacred and adorable face was spat upon.

For every bond that bound you, for every mockery and insult that was offered you, for every lie uttered against you, for every unjust sentence pronounced upon you - for all these, I bless and praise you.

All these blessings, multiplied a thousand-fold, I now offer you, my Saviour, and would willingly renew them every instant of my life. Amen.

May the Sacred Heart of Jesus in the most Blessed Sacrament be praised, adored, loved with grateful affection, at every moment, in all the tabernacles of the world, even to the end of time.

ACTS OF REPARATION
TO THE SACRED HEART

O loving heart of Jesus, prostrate before you, I wish to love you for all the coldness, irreverence, ingratitude, and sacrileges with which so many people - including myself - repay you for your wonderful love in the adorable Sacrament of the Altar.

WE TWO

I cannot do it alone;
The waves run fast and high,
And the fogs close chill around,
And the light goes out in the sky.
But I know that we two shall win in the end -
Jesus and I.

I could not steer it myself,
My ship on the roaring sea.
What of that? Another sits in my ship,
And pulls or steers with me.
And I know that we two shall come into port.
His child and he.

Coward, wayward and weak,
I change with the changing sky -
One day, eager and brave,
The next, not caring to try.
But he never gives in, and we two shall win
Jesus and I.

Strong and tender, and true,
Crucified once for me.
I know that Jesus never will change,
Whatever I do or be.
We shall finish our course, and get home at last
His child and he.

MORNING OFFERING

O Jesus, through the Immaculate Heart of Mary, I offer you the prayers, works, joys and sufferings of this day for all the intentions of your Sacred Heart, in union with the holy sacrifice of the Mass throughout the world.

PIONEER PLEDGE
IN HONOUR OF THE SACRED HEART

For your greater glory and consolation, O Sacred Heart of Jesus; for your sake, to give good example, to practice self-denial, to make reparation to you for the sins of intemperance, and for the conversion of excessive drinkers, I will abstain for life from all intoxicating drinks.

AN OFFERING IN TIME OF SUFFERING

Divine Lord, I thank you for this little cross, and I offer it to you, with your own heavy cross, for all the intentions of your Sacred Heart.

ASPIRATIONS TO JESUS MY FRIEND
By Saint Claude la Colombiére, S.J.

O Jesus, you are my true friend, my only friend. You take part in all my misfortunes; you take them on yourself; you know how to change them into blessings.

You listen to me with the greatest kindness when I relate my troubles to you, and you always heal my wounds.

I find you at all times. I find you everywhere, for you never go away. If I have to change my dwelling place I find you there wherever I go.

You are never weary of listening to me, you are never tired of doing me good.

I am certain of being loved by you no matter what happens. My goods mean nothing to you, and by bestowing yours on me you never grow poor. However miserable I may be, no one more noble or clever, or even holier, can come between you and me and deprive me of your friendship. And death, which tears us away from all other friends, will unite me forever to you.

All the humiliations attached to old age or to the loss of honour will never detach you from me. On the contrary, I shall never enjoy you more fully and you will never be closer to me than when everything seems to conspire against me and bring me down.

You put up with all my faults with extreme patience, and even my lack of fidelity and my ingratitude do not wound you to such a degree as to make you unwilling to receive me back when I return to you.

O Jesus, grant that I may die praising you, that I may die loving you, that I may die for the love of you. Amen.

Dear Jesus, help me to spread your fragrance everywhere I go. Flood me with your spirit and life. Penetrate and possess my whole being so utterly that all my life may be only a radiance of yours. Shine through me and be so in me that every soul I come in contact with may feel your presence in my soul. Let them look up and see no longer me - but only you, my Jesus.

(Cardinal Newman)

4th QUARTER

LOVE AND CONSECRATION
TO JESUS IN THE BLESSED SACRAMENT

O Jesus, hidden God, I cry to you;
O Jesus, hidden light, I turn to you;
O Jesus, hidden love, I run to you;
With all the strength I have, I worship you;
With all the love I have, I cling to you;
With all my soul, I long to be with you;
And fear no more to fail, or fall from you.

ASPIRATIONS

Sweet heart of Jesus, I implore
That I may love you daily more and more.
Sweet heart of Jesus, you are my love!
O Lord, grant that I may love you, and, as the
    sole reward of my love, grant that I may
    ever love you more and more.
May the Sacred Heart of Jesus be evermore
    loved.

PRAYER FOR GREATER LOVE OF JESUS

O my Jesus, you know well that I love you; but I do
not love you enough. O grant that I may love you
more. Your love that burns for ever, it never fails.
My God, you who are charity itself, enkindle in my
heart that divine fire which consumes the saints and
transforms them into you.   Amen.

LITANY OF THE LOVE OF GOD

Lord, have mercy on us.
Christ, have mercy on us.
Lord, have mercy on us.
God the Father of heaven,
God the Son, Redeemer of the world,
God the Holy Spirit,
Holy Trinity, one God,

Have mercy on us.

You who are infinite love,
You, who loved me first,
You, who invite me to love you,
With all my heart,
With all my mind,
With all my strength,
Above all possessions and honours,
Above all pleasures and enjoyments,
More than myself,
More than everything belonging to me,
More than all my relatives and friends,
More than all people and angels,
Above all created things in heaven and on
    earth, only for yourself,
Because you are the sovereign good,
Because you are infinitely worthy of
    being loved
Even had you not promised me heaven,
Even should I suffer want and misfortune,
    In wealth and in poverty,
    In prosperity and in adversity,
    In health and in sickness,
    In life and in death,
    In time and in eternity.

I love you, Lord my God.

LET US PRAY

My God, I love you. I desire to love you in all, and through all, and above all. Take this poor heart of mine and warm it so that all my thoughts and hopes and ambitions may centre round you.

ST. MARGARET MARY'S ACT OF CONSECRATION TO THE SACRED HEART OF JESUS

To you, O Sacred Heart of Jesus, to you I devote and offer up my life, thoughts, words, actions, pains and sufferings. May the least part of my being be no longer employed, except in loving, serving, honouring and glorifying you. Therefore, O most Sacred Heart, be the sole object of my love, the protector of my life, the pledge of my salvation and my secure refuge at the hour of my death. Be, O most bountiful heart, my justification at the throne of God. In you I place all my confidence, and convinced as I am of my own weakness, I rely entirely on your compassion. Destroy in me all that is displeasing and offensive to your pure eye. Imprint yourself like a divine seal on my heart, that I may ever remember my obligation never to be separated from you. May my name, also, I beseech you, by your tender bounty, be written in you, O Book of Life, and may I ever be a victim consecrated to your glory, ever burning with the flames of your pure love, and entirely penetrated with it for all eternity. In this I place all my happiness. This is all my desire, to live and die in no other quality but that of your devoted servant. Amen

ACT OF LOVE OF ST FRANCIS XAVIER

My God, I love you, not that I
May reign with you eternally,
Nor that I may escape the lot
Of those, O God, who love you not,
You, you, my Jesus, you for me
Did agonise on Calvary.
You bore the cross, the nails, the lance
The rabble's ignominious glance.
Unnumbered griefs, unmeasured woes,
Faintings and agonising throes,
And death itself, and all for me,
A sinner and your enemy.
And shall not then your love cause me,
Most loving Jesus, to love thee?
Not that in heaven I may reign,
Nor to escape eternal pain,
Nor in the hope of any gain;
But as, O Jesus, you love me,
So do I love, and will love thee,
Because you are my king, my Lord,
Because, O Jesus! You are God.

ACT OF CHARITY

O my God, I love you with my whole heart and
above all things, because you are the supreme good
and worthy of all my love. I am sorry for having
displeased your infinite goodness by my sins. I
desire to do your holy will, and to love you more
and more. For the love of you, I will love my
neighbour as myself.

ASPIRATIONS TO THE SACRED HEART

Love of the heart of Jesus, inflame my heart.
Charity of the heart of Jesus, flow into my heart.
Strength of the heart of Jesus, support my heart.
Mercy of the heart of Jesus, pardon my heart.
Patience of the heart of Jesus, grow not weary
of my heart.
Kingdom of the heart of Jesus, be in my heart.
Wisdom of the heart of Jesus, teach my heart.
Zeal of the heart of Jesus, consume my heart.

THE BLESSING

O my Jesus, fountain of inexhaustible benediction, you blessed the apostles before you ascended into heaven. Bless me also, and with your presence sanctify me.

Bless my memory, that it may always remember you.

Bless my understanding, that it may always think of you.

Bless my will, that it may never seek or desire that which may be displeasing to you.

Bless my body and all its actions.

Bless my heart with all its affections.

Bless me now and at the hour of my death.

Bless me in time and in eternity, and grant that your most sweet blessings may be to me a pledge of eternal happiness.

Bless all people, the faithful.

Bless my dear ones.
Bless everyone I love, and everyone to whom I owe my gratitude, and bring me and them to rest in your Sacred Heart for ever. Amen.

SHORT ACTS OF CONSECRATION TO THE SACRED HEART

O Sacred Heart of Jesus, I consecrate to you myself and all that I have - my body, my soul, my work, my home, and all those dear to me. Take charge of and bless me and mine and bring us all to you.

ACT OF CONSECRATION TO THE BLESSED SACRAMENT

I, ..., the servant of Jesus Christ, acknowledging my unworthiness, but confiding in divine grace, consecrate and devote myself with all my heart, with all my soul, with all my strength to the worship and adoration of our Lord Jesus Christ, really, truly and substantially present in the Most Holy Sacrament for the love of all.

Confirm in me, O my God, that which your grace has wrought. O Mary, blessed Mother of Jesus and my tender Mother also, love me as your child, direct me in Jesus' service so that I may be pleasing in his sight, and may serve him worthily during my life, and after my death have the happiness of praising and loving him with you throughout eternity. Amen.

ACT OF CONSECRATION TO BE MADE BEFORE A REPRESENTATION OF THE SACRED HEART

My loving Jesus, out of the grateful love I have for you and to make reparation for my unfaithfulness to grace, I give you my heart and I consecrate myself totally to you and with your help I propose never to sin again.

O Sacrament most holy,
O Sacrament divine,
All praise and all thanksgiving
Be every moment thine.